ANATOMY OF A BROKEN SOUL

written by
sehej pawar

inspired by Halsey's *I Would Leave Me If I Could*

For Ms. Harter—

You have inspired me to write this poetry book with all your endless support by starting the poetry unit in drama class and making me feel safe sharing my poetry with the whole class. Thank you for coming out to my first-ever open mic where I shared my poems for the first time, Thank you for being my inspiration and encouraging me to write and share my story. I will never forget.

For Andrew—

Because you pushed the poetry unit to be done in class, I want to thank you because it was a chance for me to share my work instead of keeping it to myself.

For Ms. White and Ms. Devo—-
I loved writing in your classes and thank you for letting me share some of it with you.

For Lillian, Nick, and Quincy—
For inspiring me.

For my parents—
Thank you for everything you have taught me in my life and for supporting me no matter what.

Table of Contents:

you are not alone

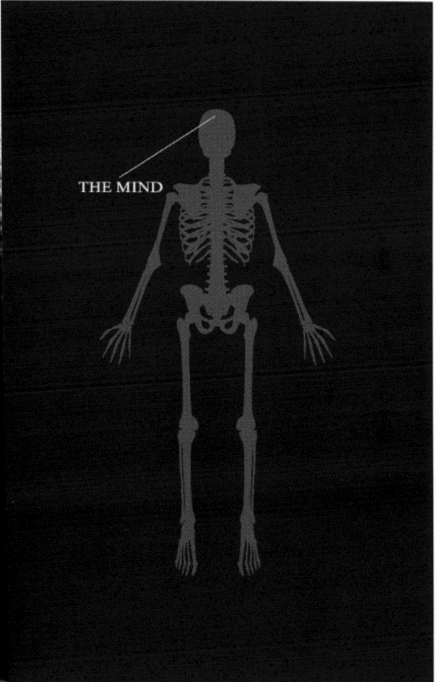

THE MIND

DEATH

Sitting in my room at night
dark, cold, just the light of my phone
listening to music with my eyes closed.
All I hear is the dial tone,
my mind goes
I'm gonna die.
I'm gonna be old.
I'm gonna be saggy ME!
I'm gonna be ugly.
I'm gonna be gray.

My heart turns dark quickly like a loss of electricity at
night.
My mind goes to places where it shouldn't go.
My little hell is located on the top of my brain.
My screams take over my whole body.
I'm already dying?
monsters, ghosts, and immortals laughing at me so happy
to see a comedy series
Is this Only Murders In The Building? This isn't the first
episode.

When will the demons stop eating me alive?
When people ask me are you ok? I say I'm fine
but I'm not fully satisfied.
If this was a horror movie you'd stab me
1 2 3 times and I'd be deceased…

But they say I'm going to turn into some wild
beast…
But this isn't a movie, it's the director's cut
unreleased,
which they don't get to see.

Caution tape wrapped around my brain,
police car sirens ringing in my head.
These delusions I love.
I find them amusing
because sometimes I don't want to live
but I'm too scared to die.
911 what's your emergency?
Hello?

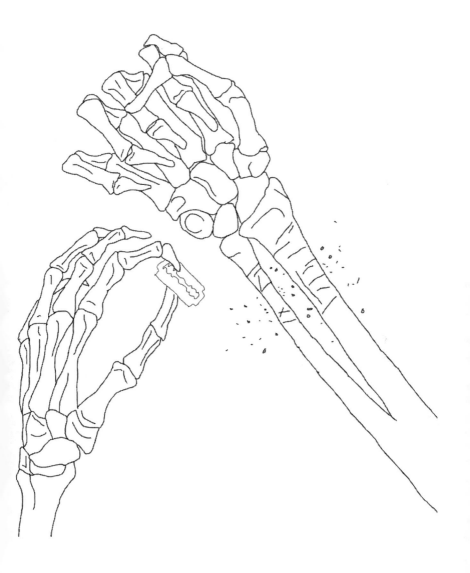

15

WHO ARE THEY?

THEY are my worst enemies…
THEY are the monsters…
that live in my bed
THEY are the ones that
keep me up at night…
THEY are the ones that
never believed in me…
THEY are the ones that
hate seeing me exist…
THEY is me…

KING

How can I control a kingdom
if my mind is the king?

Begging me to follow rules.
I don't want to play this
fairytale anymore.

SUNSETS

Sunsets are just hopes
that I make it past the
thunderstorms in my
life without the rain
drowning me.
I can hear the angels
sing already.

IT'S NOT THAT DEEP

I have done some things that
I can't escape.
I try to escape this pool
where I'm drowning, 20 feet under,
as I hear the voices telling me…

"It's not that deep Sehej."

INGREDIENTS THEY USE AT THE BAKERY

1/2 cup of overthinking
add a squeeze of tears minus the dripping

1/4 teaspoon of laziness or that's what they say I
am
don't forget to add a drop of melatonin for
sleepless nights: spray with Pam.

In a separate bowl mix
together anxiety and unwanted thoughts
crack a few feelings of loss and emptiness
mix with a whisk.

Add the wet and dry ingredients together
and mix using the addiction you have to your
phone cause that's the thing you really trust the
most right?

Now the secret ingredient…
Sprinkle in a tablespoon of thoughts of ending it
all because I would never kill myself,
I'm too afraid to die,
but say iv never thought about it
yeah, that'll be a lie.

Put it in the oven for 18 years in counting.
Make sure to use hopelessness when getting it out, you
don't want to burn yourself.

Top it off with questions in your head
and there you have it,
you just used ingredients to make sehej…

I'M JUST A KID

"You're just a kid."
"You won't understand."
"You're too small to know."
"You'll understand when you're older."

I'm now
older,
wiser,
and bigger.
Why do they think so low
of a child who wants to
understand?

LIFETIME OF MISERY

I wish I just left and never came back.
Move somewhere far away
so no one can find me…
Start a whole new life
without the people
who keep pulling on my strings
"their puppet."
I just want to live my life
for me
and be happy for me.
I want to pull on my
own strings
and the first step is to
escape this lifetime of
misery.

THE STARS

How much longer do I have
to keep wishing on the stars?
It's like the whole world hates me
for a living life that I want to live…
I didn't ask to be born.
I just want to be happy and
not romanticize about how
my life would be like if
I was stuck in rated PG-13 movies.

GAME OF LIFE

Why can't things just
show up for me?
I'm tired of playing this
game of life.
I'm scared that
I won't make it till the
end.
"It's your turn"
As I roll the dice hoping to win
one day.

MY LIFE IS…

Why do I always
feel alone in a room full of people?
If life's a movie then
mines the shitty sequel
that no one wants to watch.
I replay the director's cut that didn't
make it in my head.
While everyone enjoys popcorn
and seat warming,
I'm crying backstage
alone.

FAMILY GATHERINGS

When can they stop treating me
like a circus elephant in the room?
If I say something I get punished
for life.
They don't like anything I do…
and when they say
*"you're so quiet, why don't you
talk?"*,
how can I talk if you put
duck tape around my mouth?
You made me feel like
a kidnapped soul that doesn't
get to see the light
unless I serve all of them
well.
They make me hate myself
as a thundercloud sits on
top of me,
crying tears that I can't
cry at family gatherings.

PURPLE THOUGHTS

Why do I always feel sad
all the time?
Most days I can't even sleep at
night without
dreaming of someone trying
to murder me in my sleep.
Guts and gore are what the monsters
in my bed want me to live like
in my head.
Even Nyquil can't fix me unless
it's mixed with bleach
so I can leave this misery…
I call *"my life"*.
My lights are always purple,
a color I feel safe in,
but dark storms fill up inside
my walls.
Sometimes
I hurt myself to make sure I exist
and I pinch myself to make sure I am real.

I want to leave these dark storms
in my head and fly through lilac skies,
as I see the world through a
lavender lens instead of my human
eye that covers the world in violet
which makes me depressed.
I want to live in a world where
I have purple thoughts,
instead of the ones that make me
want to end it all.

TRAFFIC LIGHTS GIVE ME ANXIETY

I'm still shocked that I made it
this far in life….
From the crying, to
screaming in the middle of the
night,
to going past the yellow light.
But I question
how much longer will
I be able to cross the green light
without it turning red
and I just leave
leave
leave
leave this
place…

3:00 AM

It's 3:00 AM
and I woke up before
the demons that live in the bed.
Maybe this is my time to escape
the ones that haunt me at night…
But I have to fight the ones
that live in my head.

TEARS OF LILITH

Only she could keep an eye out for me.
Tell me what's going on outside the prison I
locked myself into.
I'm afraid of being alone at night
but not her.
Her eyes can see through the dark and dirty.
Mine block parts of reality at age 18,
how could she see the unseen?
Red tears dripping down her face,
creating a pool of death.
She had me wrapped around her neck
like that tight choker, she wore.
I made everything in sight get driven away,
made friends with the demon,
but I guess I'm one myself.
When she gave me her eyes
I too cried tears of Lilith.

I AM ANGRY BECAUSE OF MY DAD

I am angry because of my dad,
because when I was a kid he would
weave words in my mind that can't
get unknotted.
Chills still go down my spine.

I am angry because of my dad,
because I can hold grudges like how I hold in my
emotions
and it feels like a waterfall going up instead of
down.
A feeling I can't describe without my thoughts set
on *"explosion"*

I am angry because of my dad.
I can choose to stop but I ignore it,
my sister says I even have his snore.

I can also come home and sleep
but God is testing me.
I'm close to turning 20.
I have so much more to learn from a man.

So the real question I ask myself every night
is, am I angry because of my dad?
or
angry at myself?

Maybe one day I'll choose to answer,
But for now, I'll keep playing
God's game.

RETAINER'S

*they hurt my mouth, I can't say the letter S without
accidentally saying SH!T.*

What I told my orthodontist when she asked,
*"Why don't you wear your retainers?
that's no excuse. Your teeth need to be perfect."*

What the world around me has told me ever since
I came out of my mom's womb.

She tells me, *"Let's not get into this right now...
let's re-mold you to see if they still fit."*

Nobody can wear my retainers,
they are designed to fit perfectly for me
and me only.
Every gap, every crevice in my mouth.
So why don't I ever feel my mind fits this teenage
dream phase that everyone is supposed to have?

When I put them on I think of all the
life's mistakes I have made in my past
not much more than the last.

*"The retainers help keep you from creating empty
spaces."*
How do I tell her that's not true?
It doesn't close my emptiness or my gaps,

it opens up spaces in my mind to let the monsters in and tell me that I forgive too easily, I fuck up everything around me, and I don't deserve to be happy.

I'm sorry that I hold grudges, just like how I wish I could still hold my mom's hand.
Growing up is like a mouthful of cavities, coming in to attack every piece of my sweet childhood dreams.

Suicidal thoughts sitting in my unopened glass cup with my retainers floating to the top.
Begging me to put them back on.

I did try putting them on once…
I really did.

It was the past trying to hold on to me again.
Biting down,
baring the pain in my mouth,
a pair of plastic that supposedly protects
your perfect teeth every day and night.
The day is when my demons go away, and the night is when my mind takes over my whole body.

Thank you braces…

DEAD BODIES

One day I decided to cave in and let the monsters
that live inside of me take full control over me.
We were gliding through my mind where you can
feel the skylines buzzing like a cry for help.
They took me to the graveyard where all my
memories lie.
Tombstones covered with dirt and grime,
cobwebs on every single corner of your eye.
An unopen casket with my name on it.
I cried for help but not even my happiest memory
could have saved me.
I guess I am another dead body with memories
that haunt me.

WORDS THAT HURT

I wear black shirts
so my body looks skinnier
and so other people won't
taunt me with words they called me
when I was a kid.
"you're fat"
"lose weight."
Words that still linger in my
mind till this day.
I wish I could help my
younger self and tell
him everything's going to
be fine.
They broke him
and now I visit his grave
apologizing with tears coming
down my face.

FAT

"You're fat" has always been a saying ever since I
was a little kid.
No, you're "handsome."
No, you're a "prince."
No Mom I'm fat
I stopped eating as I got older.
Looked in the mirror and hated who was standing
in front of me.
I screamed, I cried,
sleepless nights, and food only 2 bites.
When can they start saying I'm skinny?
When can my face, cheeks, stomach, arms, and
legs be "skinny" enough to make them happy?
To call me
a handsome prince.
It started when I was six
7, goes to 11, 12, 13.
13 is when I looked in the mirror again
and said sorry.

I'M SORRY

I'm sorry for being locked in my room all day.
I can't help that the demons in my head beg me to stay.
I'm sorry for not talking.
I can't help that I fear what I'm going to say which turns
out to be a whole lot of nothing.
I'm sorry for not picking up Facetime calls.
I can't help it that the monsters have other plans
and I'm sorry to myself for thinking that no one likes me.

IN LOVING MEMORY

In loving memory of the son who locks himself in
his room blasting music.
Loves to greave alone because he doesn't give a
shit about his family right?
Nor they gave a damn about him.
Tears dropped down all their faces but
a laugh comes out of me.

In loving memory of the friend who stops hanging
out with the others because they say
"you've changed, we want the old you back"
but in reality, it was them who never realized how
much he was actually hurting inside.
Memorable posts are being posted everywhere but
a smirk shows on my face.
As my eyes roll back until I see the hell out of my
mind.

In loving memory of the son who would sit in his parent's room to have some company,
talk about his life with his mom,
eat dinner with the family sitting on that one chair on the left side.
The chair he called his own.
Tears dripping down my face but
a laugh comes out of them.

In loving memory of the friend who would stay up all night, talking to his friends about the future,
a car full of friends driving around.
It turned into a casket full of flowers brought to the front where everyone gets to see him one more time.
posting the present memories everywhere but a light shows inside my mind.
As I open my eyes to see my heaven flash back to reality.

GROWING OLDER

As I grow older,
wrinkles on my forehead
will appear,
my hands will puff up and
white hair will cover my
scalp like roses that
bloom in June.
I will start seeing the
world less.
It's crazy how we start in
our mother's
wombs
and end in a casket.
Where each rose petal
falls down
one by one,
a countdown for when
I rebloom.

TO THE PEOPLE I USED TO KNOW

I shouldn't let the people
I used to know to ruin my mood.
It's not their fault honestly.
I'm the one going through
old text messages
and scrolling all
the way back in my
camera roll
for photos that make
make me smile.
But it slowly turns
into watery eyes
and thoughts
that I will never
have those
texts and photos
of us laughing
ever again.

KINGS OF THE PLAYGROUND

In the 6th grade, I had a wish to grow up fast.
I wanted to be an adult so badly that I would
search on Google,
"how to become an adult fast."
6th grade was also where the neighborhood kids
would meet at the park across from my house.
We would play sharks and lava on the playground.
Don't even get me started on those intense 4
square games where everyone had the desire to be
king!
We were all kings of the playground.
Made up our own rules during the game of tag.
If you get caught during capture the flag you get
pinched. *(Come on kids had some sort of violence
in games) it made us kids.*
The jail base during cops and robbers was the new
climbing spider.

The web I got caught in as I got older.
Sharks and lava turned into running away from the monsters that live in my bed.
Bouncing the ball to get to king in four square was really just an act because you can't rule outside the square.
"Tag you're it" to be the one who gets scared of life because it's a game you have to play.
Try making your own rules now.
Trying to capture happiness at the end is a lie because instead of getting pinched I get punched with delusions of how my future is going to play out.
Jail is looking like a place where I can be alone.
I might have to rob the store in my brain called *"the mind of sehej"* to be free.
Can I go back to becoming the king of the playground with those friends I haven't seen?
In the 12th grade, I wish I never wished to grow up...

FOLLOW THE WHITE RABBIT

I'm following the white rabbit into the world
of my dreams.
But I'm chasing my delusions,
a fantasy
that I cry for too
be my reality.

DREAMS

I'm the same 6 feet tall boy in my dreams,
but i'm happy that no one knows my name here.
The clouds here are lavender-high
with castles that buzz sunlight low.
Through the city of dreams,
people here smile
a little too much,
something i'm not used to.
I wish I could live here
without the void I get from reality.
But I remember everything here is just
made up of fairytales and delusions,
something I choose to believe,
until the nightmares come in and burn this
place to the ground.
I'm back at square one
at 3:00 am at night.

Everything was fake.

Maybe one day my dreams will be real.

CRYING IN A SUNFLOWER FIELD

I'm standing alone in a sunflower field.
The golden light shining on me,
you can hear the birds singing so beautifully,
and the clouds are Egyptian blue.
The angel cries
and the devil a blood-red moon.
As I'm running away from being
chased by the images in my head.
I tripped and fell so they could eat me alive
but they're just my delusions that want to bloom
in the sunlight.
Why did the sun stop shining on me?
Why are the clouds dark grey?
Why are the birds screaming?
I cry walking through the graveyard.
I wish it was the sunflower field
from my dreams.

FEEL LIKE A KID AGAIN

The past is gone
and the future is
so much closer.
I'm to young to let my
childhood dreams die.
I will do anything to
feel like a kid again.

anything.

I DON'T WANT TO BE PRESENT ANYMORE

I can't even look at the future ahead of me
without looking at the scars the past has on me.
I don't want to be present anymore.

LISTENER FRIEND

I enjoy being the listener friend.
When my friends tell me whatever
is on their mind,
I agree or disagree.
They tell me about their problems
and I listen
but I don't share mine.
I'm not a talkative friend
I'm the friend that locks
inner pain inside so
no one else has to go through it
but me.
I'm the friend that keeps
my worries and struggles
inside my head
to give my mouth a rest.
Sorry, sometimes I feel like a
car accident that everyone slows down
to see.
I enjoy being the listener friend,
so I can prevent a car accident from happening
again.

IF I WAS IN CINDERELLA

If I was in Cinderella I would of
wished for a different life,
where i'm allowed to run in a field of roses
instead of stuck in a bouquet, waiting to die.

I don't care for new clothes and a princess.
I just want to have my own happy ever after.
I'm tired of doing their
  "chores"
washing my mouth out with soap because
some days I speak too much
and get locked in a tower for doing so.

The key is in their pocket,
but I don't care for an escape.
I break glass
for noise where
my life isn't that quiet.

The shoe fits but I don't fit
in this world.
I cry,
I scream,
People haunt me.
The birds are afraid
when they hear me sing,

The mice have tried to help me
escape.

How do I tell them,
"it's not you
it's me."

Fairy Godmother, please
bibbidi bobbidi me out of
this misery
and give me a happy ever after
where I can run through a field of roses,
and hear the birds sing,
and for me to not be afraid
of what life has to offer me.

THE PEOPLE I USED TO KNOW

I shouldn't let the people
I used to know ruined my mood.
It's not their fault honestly.
I'm the one going through
old text messages
and scrolling all
the way back in my
camera roll
for photos that make
me smile.
But it slowly turns
into watery eyes
and thoughts
that I will never
have those
texts and photos
of us laughing
ever again.
They come into you're life
at your worse
and
leave at your best.
I'm back to the worst.

DOLLAR STORE RECEIPT

Let me tell you all the things I bought from the dollar
store.
I bought fake flowers in front of the store
because real ones don't deserve me $1.25.
I bought 3 rolls of tape so I can triple-tape the holes in
my past shut. Oh shit, it's not really working $3.75.
I bought a toy phone because sometimes it's too hard to
trust mine $1.25.
I bought a box of Kleenex for all the times i've been left
crying in my room with the doors locked, I'm still looking
for the keys $1.25.
I bought a lighter, trying to burn the past but somehow
they still found a way to roll those ashes and smoke me
back in $1.25.
I bought fake money so I can buy fake things to satisfy
my delusions. Sorry, sometimes I do want to die $1.25.
I bought a mini-moon lamp because my mom said *"it will
light up your dark room"* but my lights stay purple.
Purple a color I actually feel safe in $1.25.
I bought 5 packs of batteries to recharge myself
throughout the week because sometimes I feel fine acting
like a machine,
but on the weekends trust me, you won't even see me
$6.25.
Would you like a bag for 50 cents?
Sure! I need something to carry myself in.
Your total is $18.
no tax?

GOING THROUGH SOMETHING

Sunday was ordinary you know.
Eat, sleep, shower, and lock yourself in your room
for the rest of the day.

Woke up Monday, I think I need a new life.
Brush my teeth and hope the future is fine.
Maybe crying doesn't help anymore.
Or maybe life just doesn't mean anything.
So i'm going to get a tattoo that I might regret
later and a piercing that might sting like pain in
life that lingers.

I really want to die but it's only Tuesday.
I don't give a fuck about my life.
Yes, i'm out of my mind.
I'm going through something.

I'm fucked up but it's only Wednesday.
It's really been 365 days that I just wasted all
because iv been stuck at some place in my head.
Traffic that doesn't want to move.
The GPS tracker says i'm going to be home soon.

liar

Look here I am standing here Thursday,
bruises on my body, and have no idea where they
come from.

Scratches that still give me chills down my spine, phones
ringing asking me when I can come home.
I can't die tomorrow.
I'm busy Friday so
you just have to wait.
I'll let you know if my plans change.
I must be going through something
or maybe my life just doesn't mean anything
to me anymore.

I FUCKING HATE PARTIES

Party full of red cups on the floor,
the couple making out in the corner,
vomit on the boy's shoulder on the left of me,
broken pieces of a chandelier.
I can't take this anymore.
Places full of faces where I don't fit in at all.
They aren't there for the party
and not when it ends.
Everyone's laughing, drinking, and dancing.
While my heads down scrolling through my
phone wishing I wasn't here in the first place.
So I left the party.
I didn't tell anybody because I hate saying
goodbye.
Raise your hand if you noticed!
Why do normal things make me so sad?

Wait so if tequila shots
and cigarettes
flavored air,
no-not just vape pens
midnight parties
and random sex
car rides and parties make my friends smile
and laugh
but make me depressed.
Are we really supposed to live a life like that?
It makes me wonder if anything will make me happy.
I fucking hate parties.
Call me if you want to help me with therapy.

CONVERSATIONS

It's 1 a.m. and I'm staring at my window
admiring the stars sparkling up new dimensions
being created in my mind.

He starts talking to me.
I have these conversations that make me want to
scream.
Can it wait till I turn 20?

Now it's 2 a.m. and I'm staring at my window.
He won't let me escape.
I'm going 80 on a 60 highway.
I keep questioning if I should hit the brake.
Why did he suddenly turn 8?

It's 3 a.m. and I'm staring at myself in the mirror.
I need to talk face-to-face with the person I fear.
Why do I question everything?
Can you let me place my ace?
I'm 18 I don't want to be bait for others.

Different versions of him keep talking to me every night.
I don't want to die,
I just want these conversations to leave my head.
I already have monsters in my bed.
My biggest enemy is me.

Maybe one day I'll see the light,
ride through a blood-red sunset that only I know of,
so I can make these conversions in my head stop making
me feel all alone.

THE HEART

ONE DAY

I deleted our photos from
my camera roll
so I can stop going through them
on random days
when I think about you.
I unfollowed you on Instagram
so I can stop seeing your stories
everyday
but,
I couldn't block your number
from my contacts.
Because I hope to see
a message from you one day.

LOSE MYSELF

If you're gonna lie,
why didn't you at least try?
Because when I'm loving you,
I lose myself every day and night.

NOT READY

I'm used to having people
leave my life
but something about you
still lingers in my mind.
I don't think I'm
ready to let you leave.

as I erased this message from
your texts
not ready to send.

CRUSH

I love how you started off
as my crush,
but ended up
crushing the thing I beat
for you.

PROMISES ARE LIES

I stopped believing in promises.
You made them for comfort
but made me cry.
Don't think I will ever forget
the times you lied
because our love will forever
remember.

THE HOODIE

You know it's done when
she stops wearing his hoodie
on a typical Tuesday night.
She says,
*"I can't smell our memories
anymore."*
He stops wearing the hoodies
she wore.
He doesn't even remember
that she has the hoodie
that has the
promises,
trust,
and the
future plans
but now she keeps it in
the back of her head
where those memories won't
hurt
the way she was hurt by him.

LONELY NIGHTS

I fell in love with you at a place
that makes me think of you
every night.
Now it's the last place
I'll never fall in love
for the first time.
There's nothing to think
about on these
lonely nights.

HEY YOU…

Hey you…
You seem different.
You seem happy without me,
and seeing you smile without me,
seeing you laugh without me,
seeing you drive without me,
makes me feel happy
that someone else is making you
happier.

I'm sorry I couldn't make you
happier.

HAUNTING

I can't sleep at night
because the thought
of all the things we could
of done still, haunts me
at 3:00 am.

FIRST DAY

Today is the first day that I
chose an outfit to wear
without calling you.
Today is the day that I
chose where to eat
without thinking about
your favorite place to eat.
Today is the day that I
chose what movie to watch
without asking you.
I ended up finding
things about myself
after losing you,
so I hope the next person
that chooses me
gets the better version
that you can't ruin.

I CAN'T ESCAPE YOU

Why do you still haunt me
at night?
When I still feel your presence
near me.
You already broke my heart into 2,
Why do you want to break me?

TRY

I wish the things I
loved about you
can now make me
love myself.

Or at least try.

STRAWBERRY MILKSHAKE

You know it hurts when
we cross paths with one another
and act like we never met.
Or when someone asks me if I
knew you
and I smile as memories start
playing back in my mind.
As I respond,
 "I did."
Or when I'm eating at our
favorite restaurant and I get
a milkshake with just one straw
instead of 2.
These flashbacks
hurt but what hurts the
most is knowing
that you will never be mine
again.
As I sip the strawberry milkshake
you would share with me
alone.

EXCUSES

I hope you know that
promises you
made with me are
excuses for not wanting to be
there in my life
as I'm lost in the love
of all your lies.

SONGS ABOUT YOU

Call me crazy but
I have a playlist of songs
that make me think about
you.
The ones you listened to with me.
The ones we sang on the top
of our lungs in the car.
The ones you posted me
to on your stories.
The ones you posted
him on as well.
Now you sing those songs
in his car,
while I listen to them
in my room alone
thinking of you.

"GREAT" FAIRY TALE

I picked someone that
was going to break my heart.
Shatter me into pieces
with wounded cuts that
won't heal.
You made me feel
crazy thinking it was
all my fault,
but I guess
all "great" fairy tales
come to an end right?

I HOPE

I hope you are somewhere
happier without me
because we were supposed
to be forever, but I guess you lied.
We made plans,
shared dreams.
We said forever
but I guess we lied.

GHOST

How much longer will
you make the wounds
you cut with your heart sting?
Every day and night
I hear your voice
through my heartbeat,
like a ghost that I can't
see but feel every memory
attached that ends up
haunting me.

HEART STEALER

The worst part of it all
wasn't you leaving me
with tears,
but stealing my heart
and breaking it.
To make me never love
someone as much as I loved
you
again.

I MISS YOU

Every single day
I think about texting you
a *"hey"* or
"I miss you"
but people do say
that if you love someone
let them go and they will
eventually, come back to you.
But I want you with me
here
now
I miss you.
the things I wish
I could do with you.

I TALK ABOUT YOU ALL THE TIME.

I talk about you all the time.
From your beautiful blue eyes
to the way you laugh
at my jokes that aren't even funny.
I tell everyone about the
movie we watched together
where you held my hand
at a jump scare,
and when you gave me a
tissue when our favorite character
died.
I talk about you all the time
to avoid the pain in my heart
of you never coming back.
It's hard to move on when I still feel like
you're here.

SAFE & SOUND

If you're gonna leave,
leave me in the shape
you found me.
Smiling,
happy,
loving,
safe and sound.
Don't leave me
in the shape you left me
in.
Crying,
aching,
from
leaving me
with a broken heart.

I HOPE YOU HURT MORE

I shouldn't be the one
that's hurting this much.
I hope you hurt more than
I did.
I hope you dream about me.
I hope your little sister turns out
to be nothing like you.
I hope you cry in the bathroom
reminiscing about the good
times you had with me.
I hope your heartaches
and your head hurts
thinking about
the promises
you made.
wait
they were all lies.

Honestly, I wish nothing but
happiness for you.

THE THINGS I STILL HAVE

I still have all the birthday
posters you made.
I have them pinned on
my wall and stare at them
everyday.
I still have the stuffed bear
you gave me.
I hold it and it
makes me think I'm
holding you.
I still have the key chain
of the Eiffel Tower you gave me.
I remember when you
said we would go to Paris
in the future.
I still have your name
in my contacts without
the heart.
I can't seem to get rid
of the things you gave me
and never will.

SHE DOESN'T KNOW WHO I AM

She doesn't know who
I am,
but I hope she does.
I want to win her a carnival
bear so bad.
I want to hold her hand
as we walk on the beach
with the breeze in our hair.
I want to cook her a new
meal I've been working on.
I want to see her smile
every day.

She doesn't know who
I am.
it's not her fault
but I don't want her.
I need her.

MY HEART

Why is my heart wired out of
place?
Is my heart plugged in
wrong?
Why was I born
with a heart
that's nothing but
broken?

I ACCIDENTALLY CALLED YOU

I can't believe I accidentally
called you.
Half of me wanted to
and the other half was terrified.
I just wanted to hear your voice
for another time.
The rings of the phone
were only hopes that
you would answer.
How stupid am I…
Accidentally calling you.
After the 3rd ring, i hung up,
but I'm still waiting
for a call back from you.

LOVE MAKES PEOPLE CRAZY

I don't think I'll ever die
for love, but when it comes
to you, I'll let you take my
heart and break it for
what I care.
But don't shoot
for the memories we
had.

HONEY

She was sweet like
honey, but I could taste
the bitterness of the lies
she said.
The taste of blood
lingering in my mouth
because it felt
like she just killed
a man
and took his heart
without warning.
She was sweet like
honey
but stung like a
blood-sucking bee
on the heart.

FOUND WHAT YOU WERE LOOKING FOR?

Find another guy who says
I love you
I meant it.
Find another guy
that will love you
as much as I did.
Find another guy
that can make you smile
on random days
like I did.
Find another guy
that holds your hand
when you walk,
now I walk alone.
Find another guy that
you can stay up calling,
now I stay up thinking
about you.

I hope you found what
you were looking for but
you won't get another me.

MAYBE I SHOULD BE MORE LIKE HIM

how does he kiss you
can I try it too?
I hear you talking
about him in your sleep
and the taste of your kiss
is making me want
to burn all
the poems iv written
about you
because
you got me talking about
him in my sleep now.
I bet he's the one.
I can smell his cologne
on you and
man
I get it.
I can feel my heartache
every time you remember
his hand holding
yours.
Maybe I should be more like
him.
Your #1 right?

DAYS OF THE WEEK

I see you in the
hallway with him
and I pretend I didn't see.
I walk by with my
eyes glued to the floor
I wish it was me.
The way he waits for
you after class
as you hold his hand
and I'm suffering
as I see you two
every single school day,
thinking why him
and not me?
Every Monday -Friday
haunts me.

HATED

I love how you
unfollowed me but
still follow the ones we hated.
It makes me wonder
if I was considered
hated by you
as i unfollowed you
to
thinking
"was our love
a lie?"

WHEN IT'S OVER

You know it's over when she
unfollows his family members
on Instagram
but before that she deleted
the highlight of the stories
of them 2 together.
As well as his name from
her bio.
That was the easy part.
She still has to
delete all their photos
together of them kissing,
the feeling of her hands
touching his,
the memories she
made.
The thought of him stays
so when is it really over?

THE FUTURE WITH YOU

I've come to conclusion
that we're all gonna die
one die
but I want to die with you.
Grow old together as we
dance in the living room
while our kids laugh,
have you sleep next to
me on the bed,
get married, buy a house,
eat dinner, and get the dog we always wanted.
why did you have to
leave me so soon?

I WISH I COULD SEND YOU THIS

I'll be alone if I
can't be with you.
You make me smile.
You took half my heart.
You are the one I think about
when I wake up in the morning.
You make me laugh and smile.
You took half my soul.
You are the one I see
growing old with.
Burning the food in the kitchen
as our kids laugh.
But I'll be alone,
if I can't be with you.

INSTAGRAM STORIES

I know we moved on
from each other
but some days I still think
about you
and get scared when you
post a story on Instagram
thinking you found someone
new.
It's just a photo of you
but one day that day will come
when you post him
and share memories on
your Instagram stories
as I watch them.
Remembering the stories
you posted of me.

YOU WIN

I go to sleep
and dream about you.
Do you think I want to?
No cause I hate
how you win without
even knowing.

CANDLELIGHT

He was covering the
light of the candle
as he was trying to
keep the love between
them alive.
She tried many times
to blow the light
as each bit of his
soul turned to ash
where she smokes
him right back up.
He did what he had to
do but she blew the light out.

YOUR NAME

Your name is something
I will never forget.
The way it made me smile
when I would say it.
Now I can't even bear
to say it without
a tear coming
down my eye
or the thought of
me never finding
another you ever again.
It's like a spell that won't cast.
It's the curse of me never saying it again.

PHONE CALLS WITH YOU

I'm sitting in my room
alone wishing
I was calling you
like we used to call
every single day till 4
in the morning.
The way you smiled
on camera made me think
I would have you forever
but I just have screenshots
of funny faces you made on
facetime and just thoughts
of who can I call now
if it isn't
as I'm this close
to press the green button
to see your face again.

POSTS OF HIM

I hate how you post him
like nothing happened
between us.
He gets posted every month
while I get memories
of the stuff we did together.
Now you do it with him
with a smile on your face
and tears on mine.
How could you post him
to songs you posted me
to?

MAX

I hope Max kisses you
well and tells all his friends
about your perfect smile
like I did.
I hope Max gives you his
hoodie on days when you
feel cold
like I did.
I hope Max shares your
favorite strawberry
milkshake that we used
to get with 2 straws.
I hope Max holds your hand
and tells you he loves you
just like I did.

RESENTFUL

Heard you found someone
new
who watches movies
with you, till 33,
holds your hand
as you walk down the street.
says *"I love you"*
and act like it's real.
Share memories with you
while others send me
screenshots.
made promises with him
let's see if you keep them.

I don't give a fuck

yeah, I do.

LIKE HIM

I wore earrings and
combed my hair back
so I can look more like him
but it didn't get your attention.
I kept the same cologne
hoping you can smell
it a mile away
but I should come to
terms that I will never
be like him
and you will never
be mine again.

OUR DREAMS

At the end
you and I were never
supposed to live out
our dreams
together like we
promised.

AUGUST

Your birthday month
thinking about the times
when I would stay up till 12
to be the first to wish you a
happy birthday
but it's also the month
where I think about you the most
as you left me
for him.
You spent your birthday with me
but now you spend it with him.

Happy Birthday I still
care about you.

As I delete this message
at 12
wanting to send
but
he's probably the one
who wished you first.

CAR CRASH

The time you picked me
up and
crashed my heart going
110 on the highway.
I don't get it
how you survived
with a smile on your face
and another man
while I was left in
a hospital with
my heart taken
and shattered into pieces
and wounds that won't
heal after the car crash.

I DON'T KNOW HOW TO LOVE ANYMORE

I don't know how to love anymore.
I gave my all to you
and I'm scared
the next person I say
I love you to
will leave me
like you did.

HIS CAR

I see you walk into
his car.
It's the white one.
You probably sing
the songs we sang
together when you sat
in mine,
share laughs
together on 1st street
as I drive alone
thinking every
white car is his.

ALL BECAUSE OF YOU

The worst part of you
leaving me was
that I can't sing the songs
you sang with me in
the car anymore.
That I can't even talk
to our same old friends
or re-watch our favorite
shows.
Now I don't even wear
the clothes you said
I looked good in.
I can't even
walk down the street
without thinking of you
walking with me.

all because of you.

FEELINGS FOR YOU

I have so many feelings
for you
but I'm scared
that you're too good for me
and will leave me
like the ones
before.

I'M GLAD YOU LEFT

I'm glad you left
because after you
left I found the person
I should have loved more…

STOCKHOLM SYNDROME

He tells her promises that he could never keep
like she was his forever.
He knows that if she leaves she will be alone from
the world.
Every day she follows him around
and keeps a smile on her face
but deep down she knows
the mistake she's made.
She makes it out most times of the day
but she's still stuck behind bars in his
beating heart.
He saw her at her
most beautiful,
her most hated,
her worst.
He pushed her out until she couldn't hold him
anymore.
She tried to save him but he closed
his car doors.
She had to break her heart
so she can escape the bars.
She loved him with all her heart
but in the end, he laughs at her
as she falls apart.

FRIENDS CAN BREAK YOUR HEART TO

Friendships that end scar your heart more than anything.

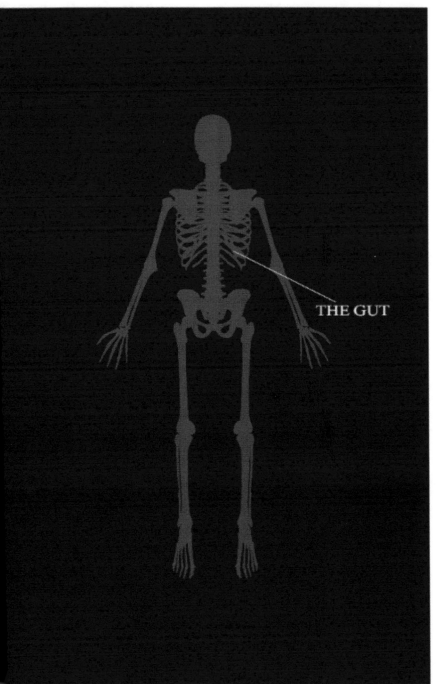

THE GUT

MY FIRST POEM

Life is like a lyric,
until you sing it.

CIRCUS

I'm standing in the middle of the circus show
trying to tame the lions with roars I have feared in
my life.
I'm dressed up as a sad clown
because I forgot how to be happy
and laugh.
It's hard to juggle these responsibilities
that life just keeps throwing at me
because I'm still on this tightrope of challenges
that growing up keeps doing to me.
I don't care.
I'm stuck on this carousel
with my clown nose red
spinning round and round
till the happy clown inside of me
tames the lion with courage.

BLACK ROSES

My favorite flowers are black roses.
they truly don't exist in nature
but they do in my head.
As every
petal holds reasons why I exist
in this world of dark shadows
that hold beautiful stories of a
boy wishing fairytales were real.
Black roses aren't real but so are the
delusions my mind starts to think of.

AN ANGEL ON FIRE

The day it finally rains is the day
I am actually happy.
My mind stopped creating these floods,
my mood is usually those metaphors you hear.
rain cloud on my head
feelings spur cats and dogs
cloudy with a chance of "happiness"
After it rains you see a rainbow
but curiosity occurs to me
saying,
"what's on the other side?"
Pot of gold, luck to money.
In my world, I hope the end of each side gives me
some sort of happiness.
But today, I don't need the 6 colors in the sky,
I need the angel's tears from up above.
Thanks to the rain,
I was an angel on fire
confronting the devil.

GREAT ESCAPE

I still have cuts that suck me deep into another side of my
mind that I don't want to be in.
A world where graveyards echo with cries from a mile
away,
tears flood resident's homes,
the sky grey with a smell
of poisonous smoke that
makes you wish you could die.
But I'm trying to change that world
no matter what it takes,
I'm going to escape

THE WAR

The war between the demons and different versions of me took place.

1 year old me brought a pacifier in case 15 year old me said too much.

2 year old me brought an empty milk bottle to drink as he minded his own business.

3 year old me brought his favorite red blanket which he loved to share with 16 year old me.

4 year old me brought 9 fingers because he lost one in the middle of the war.

5 year old me brought a razor the same one he used when he accidentally shaved his little sister's head.

6 year old me brought nothing cause he didn't exist.

7 year old me brought a box of crayons cause he thought asking demons to color would help.

8 year old me brought a smile on his face because it was the best years of his life.

9 year old me brought hatred for the way he looked which followed all the way up till 13 year old me.

10 year old me brought the killer dance moves because it's nice to have fun once in a while.

11 year old me brought insecurities of being body shamed.

12 year old me brought a jar of tears because people can be so mean.

13 year old me brought his classes so he could see the world better.
14 year old me barely made it but he brought an imaginary knife because that's when those thoughts occurred.
15 year old me was locked in his room alone.
16 year old me brought some sort of cheerfulness and told the others *"it's going to be ok"*.
17 year old me brought a car hoping to leave this place and never come back.
18 year old me tried to bring every version of me
to fight the demons
that won't let me be free.

BLISTERS

It's the pain of my emotions that people will never understand,
no matter how hard I "dumb" down my explanations.
So I started looking through the red sunset,
listening to the transmission poles' glitchy sounds.
Like the blisters that peel reasons why life isn't worth living anymore.
Around my lips the ones in pain
stopped quivering when I felt nervous
instead, you could see how stiff they get
stiff when you ask me *"are you ok?"*
of course, I lie.
If only I could burn the demons I call mine,
but I'll only cause a fire-breathing riot if I hear
that voice in my head one more time,
because all they gave me was blisters on my hand
and reasons that are too hard to forget.

PIANO

I want to sit in a room alone
and write sad songs on the piano.
I heard from a friend of a friend
that it's easier than crying
in the dark on your bed.
I don't care for a beautiful sound
when I hit the keys.
Just something I can do
to use the words I shoot down
with a gun to be set free.
I don't know how to play the piano,
but I know what I want to say.

ANATOMY OF A BROKEN SOUL

They can cut me open,
suck the poison
from my aching soul,
throbbing to be released.
You see birds locked up in cages they call home,
cause the wild was just too much to bear with.
The expression *"butterflies in my stomach"*
turned out to be real even tho
they felt like warning signs,
as I chose to ignore them.
Just to wake up seeing the butterfly in my
stomach, cruising through the sunset
and dead once reached
the edge of the clouds.
I'm now alone… again.
They try to sew me together but there will always
be that one hole
that seems to never go away.
But i've come to the conclusion,
its my anatomical structure of a broken soul that
doesn't have a home for happiness.

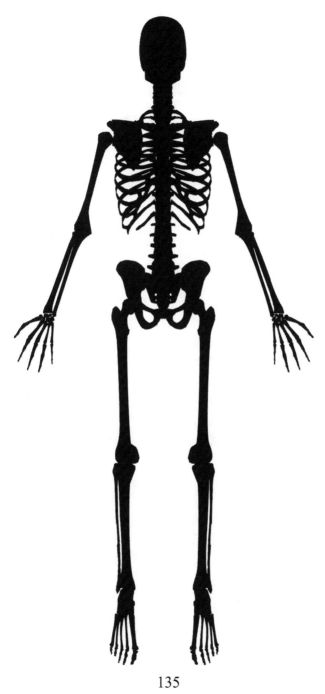

JENNIE

Jennie was a nic fiend,
most of my friends were.
While I had no business in anything in that
category.
I watched them throw up at parties and do cool
tricks with flavored air.
I was never high
but always had a good time with them.
Jennie drove a Tesla after her car got wrecked.
She drove recklessly
but always got to where she wanted to be without
a scratch.
Jennie got guys wrapped around her ring
but hated her body.
She would talk to guys to pass the time in her life.
Call them
and go on little dates in the middle of the night.
She would rant to me about a different guy every
month and how they didn't pay for her or how
their music taste sucked,
and when she hasn't called for months I would
assume she found the one.
But she was hurting inside.
I called her and asked how she does this.
how it doesn't break her heart each time she has
"fun" or if she loves them.
"I do love all of them,
more my self"
she said.

FORGIVE ME

This world isn't big enough for us to
coexist.
The little boy I was is still holding my wrist.
I don't have the energy to keep him alive anymore,
my wrist is already too sore.
As I bite my tongue hoping it kills him.
I burn his memories hoping it kills him.
I make him cry hoping he swims in the tears and goes
away,
but he says he forgives me
I wish I could to.

PAST PRESENT FUTURE

I'm so scared to find out what's gonna happen in
the future that I forget how much i've grown from
the past.
I wish I could learn how to appreciate my present
self more before I start getting scared of him.

GUTSY

I hate the people who are too gutsy.
The act of confidence on their face,
not even a nervous breath of air around them.
While I show how scared I am in any situation.
With sweat dripping down my face
like rain in late November.
When the time's change
and people break
due to darkness hovering over
me quickly.

Maybe I don't hate people who are too gutsy,
but jealous
wishing I could be
just as confidence.

MOM

My mom is the type of person who gives me the
last slice of pizza even though I could tell she
really wants it.
She starves herself so her kids can be full.

My mom worked many jobs when she came from
India to the U.S.
Factories of meat packaging,
cutting shriveled up carrots,
farming in the hot sun,
to where her back begins to ache.
Feet feel like she's walking on glass.
She doesn't care.
Working night shifts as a security
guard,
making subway sandwiches till
she sees a smile on our faces.

She doesn't go to family parties because
she's working a double shift.
She hides her pain well
but not well enough from me.

She learned english from watching
Michelle Tanner saying *"you got it dude"*
and the Berenstain Bears.
Shows i've also watched as a kid.
While my mom was gone to work,

I still remember the first time I saw her leave for work.
I was 5 and cried and cried.
Tried to wait until she came home.

Now i'm 18 and understand the struggles from the highs
and lows of my mother.
When I hear the garage door open I run downstairs to see
her face
and am grateful for the hardworking women in my life
I call my mom.

TRUTH SERUM

Go ahead and tie me up
to a chair and beat me to death
like you see in crime movies.
I don't fucking care.
Feed me truth serum
thinking I will spill my guts to you.
Not even my phone has my darkest secrets
for you to keep.
I'm not stupid enough to write down
my secrets for you to go through.
Let's see you try to tame my beast

wait...

LEAVE ME TO

I'm so tired of living a life I don't care for anymore.
I push people that care for me away
faster than how I used to respond to texts.
Group chats give me anxiety.
My friends say I only text if it something involves me.
I scream alone in my room
where no one can hear me.
I wouldn't even be angry if people left me
because i wish i could leave me to.

QUICKSAND

I'm walking through every chapter in life
and step in quicksand.
Where every cry and scream keeps pulling me
down.
My body is deep inside
but my head is out
for my mind to continue making up
these nightmares
where ghosts live in my ears
whisper different things for
the brain to overreact.
My eyes pitch black like the starting
of a new horror movie where
someone dies in the first 10 minutes.
My soul is trapped
but i'm fine drowning in quicksand.

CONTACTS COULDN'T SAVE ME

The world has always been blurry to me
as I walk through one of those childhood stories
where someone picks a path to go through the woods.
A safe longer way to get out of the forest
or a quick dangerous way to get out.
I always choose the dangerous way.
I cant see the world clearly nor do I want to
see myself making wrong mistakes
where people leave cuts
all over my broken body
for not doing anything right.
Not even contacts could save me
because when I cry in contacts,
I see the useless 18 year old
crying outside the door step
because he never wished to
to see this world
through a skeletons perspective.

dead.

MUNNI'S WORDS

"Only 2 times that your loved ones will be gathered for you, your funeral, and your wedding."

"unless you have an over the top birthday party."

ZENITH

I'm still climbing the edge of the stars
to find the place of happienes
inside my mind.
i'll call you when I reach zenith.

BLUE BOY

Inside my mind lives a boy.
His cries echo through the halls
like a dark tunnel in horror movies.
His screams shake up the melting walls,
a candle that doesn't blow out.
His heart a ticking time bomb
that's just waiting to be set off.
His dreams a disguise as old halloween
costumes in the attic where everyone's scared to
go.
His eyes flicker like lights when he wakes me
up in the middle of the night
with his tears running down
a un fixable sink.
Someone call the plumber.
The police think there's a crime scene
as his bed is filled with blood.
His tongue is on fire.
Maybe it was for the best so he can stop saying
things to me.

"Come in come in"
you won't see blue boy anymore
but you can still hear his ghost
linger inside my mind.

VAMPIRE FEELS

I always wonder how vampires feel.
They live through so much pain and agony in life
from seeing their loved ones die
and the world through a third eye,
without letting it consume them in pain.
I wonder how they do it.
I wonder how they feel
walking alone at night
thinking about the feelings
of love and lost they once had
or still do.
If their heart still beat for the ones they loved
or if their veins travel blood back to the past when their
lives were human.
I have many questions
but I wonder the most if
they love living.

BIRTHDAY

I was once a happy boy on my birthday
seeing all the balloons and decorations throughout
the hall way.
Feeling of happiness and excitement
something I miss.
I'm standing behind the table staring at my
spiderman cake,
like how I would stair at the night sky every day
wishing for a present on my birthday.
They sing me the song
and I have the biggest smile on my face.
Getting caked, pictures with hats.
Those memories I can never erase.

I'm now standing behind the table staring at my
cake.
I blow out the candles that say 18.
happy birthday to me.
As a kid I was careless with no thoughts
but i'm getting older
and scared of what the future holds.
I'm a year closer to death,
wishing it was back to my tenth.

They say I got a whole life ahead
but i'm scared to live it wrong.
It gets better they say
but what if I can't?

DREAM CATCHER

If dream catchers catch nightmares
then why do they let my good dreams slip
through a tunnel in time?
It whispers, begging me to
stay where i'm happy.
Dream catchers lie.
They still have secretes
that will stay with me till the day I die
please catch them
the ones that control my head.

BUTTERFLIES IN MY STOMACH

Butterflies come rushing in my stomach.
Something i've been used to since I was a kid
but that gut feeling,
takes a different tole on you when you began growing up.
Butterflies sting.
So do bees when you steal their honey.
How can I trust my gut again
if the butterflies were already
warning signs.

LOST INSIDE

If you ever wanna see me again
grab a paper and a pen
and draw a photo based off of memory.
My phone is somewhere looking for me.
I'm feeling kind of lonely
waiting for time to pass me by.
Nobody knows who I am
as I look in the mirror to examine
my face
and I fear the person standing in front of me.
They said these are the best years of life
but why do I feel so lost
inside?

STAINED

They think i'm in insane
but my soul is stained.
Like a coffee ring on a table without a coaster
because their meant to help the surface of a table.
Help is something that doesn't work for me.
Everyone is convincing me that i'm crazy
but do soldiers forget their battles
after seeing blood stains on the battle field?

TONGUE

Cut my tongue off
i'm scared of the words
that it's says to me.
I don't think before I speak
to help avoid the fight I have with my tongue.
When I bite down and I scream.
The truth hurts
and the secrets kill
but I have to shoot down all the words
that my tongue thinks.

PEOPLE ARE HARD TO UNDERSTAND

Can't tell if they love me
or hate me.
Or want to see me fall
off a mountain without
a ground underneath.
Somebody told me
"someones wishing for your suffering."
I think that somebody is me.

CASTLES AND PILLOWS

I built us castles with pillows.
Used play tents as roller coasters
and beds as a trampolines.
Surprised our heads didn't burst open with a river
of blood
like how we fell riding bikes
though the morning sunrise
when we lived in 3109.
We pretended to win awards and said speeches
recreating our dreams.
Wished we lived in a real castle.
I guess most of them came true.

Fights were down to happen
but we both know we can't go a day without saying
random things.
Laughing, reminiscing our memories
from 5 to 8 to 13
when I had braces
and you didn't know how to tie your shoe laces.
(still don't)
I told you once I get a car
we'll do the things they
we're afraid of us doing.
Sneaking out and going shopping.
We will forever be those 2 kids
dreaming it big
and screamimg at eachother
as long as
we still have the castle made out of pillows.

MY SISTER

My sister is the kind of person
who does tik tok dances
and takes photos of everything going on
in here life.
She wears airpods in her ear where
she blocks the world
listening to music.
She wears clothing that match her
made up aesthetic,
wears makeup
and fake eyelashes.
My sister is the kind of person
who laughs at everything.
She lives a care free life or that's what I imagine it
to be.
She doesn't care about what other people think.
If you make fun of her acne
she'll say something back.
She loves living in the moment
and keeps her wishes to herself
which is why I can never be like her.
She loves herself even without the cake on her
face
and admires the world she lives in her head
with the sad songs that start playing.
I can hear it through her ears
but not through her.

TRUSTING IN LIFE

iI don't always trust people in my life
because they tend to leave my life
like the speed of sound.
You won't even know what hit you.
But the thing I trust the most
are memories from old photographs
because they can stay with me
even if people fade from my life.

DIAPASON

I woke up one morning
and the world was frozen.
Time stopped and water hitting
the sink without a sound,
I'm alone again,
scared i'm stuck in a world
where I have no connection to anyone.
Telephone poles stay still
but you can still hear the wind
buzz with confusion.
I'm running all over town
to find someone else
but the town echos my name
a person that needs to be saved.
No one hears me scream.
No one hears me cry.
The sky is green and the
floor blue.
I'm laying down admiring
the birds in the sky,
a still picture wishing I could fly.
The flowers move
and the sun switches to the moon.
I'm walking again
and see cars that flash their headlights
with no one sitting in the drivers seat,
running thinking they are chasing me
but the only thing being chased is

me searching for someone to tell
what's going on with me.
Someone who can believe what i've seen.
I'm still in pain,
the clouds are grey ready to
release rain.
I run back to my house.
Maybe it's good to feel alone
and not hear sounds
ringing in my head.
I guess one person can believe me.

PERMANENT MARKER

I see them with my eyes closed.
I can feel the presence of all the monsters
in the room ready to attack me.
I open my eyes to show some courage
but I close them tighter.
They rip my clothes off with a knife
because scissors are said to be safer.
Can we get a nurse in the room?
I cave in because my body can't handle to get
back up and fight.
My minds tired
and my eyes ran out of water to
see the waterfall flowing down.
I look straight up to the ceiling,
pretending I can see stars to wish my death
before they kill me.
I knew I was going to die but never have thought
my mind was the one going to do it.
My hands shake and my legs numb from being
strapped to my bed.
I open my eyes wide and see them holding
weapons and torches.
What did I do wrong?
I guess it's time.
I don't have a final goodbye.
I feel sharp pinches on my body
not from knives or swords
but from permanent markers,
as each one writes words that haunt me to death.

Blood leaks through my body but dries
the words.
I'm covered with permanent marker,
never knew that words would be the death of me.

SCARED OF FEELING

I'm scared of feeling happy.
Right after that split second of happiness around
me,
the world shifts for the worst.
I'm scared of feeling
emotions,
if i'm not doing it right
for the world to approve.

I WONDER WHY

I woke up with a smile on my face.
I'm happy?
I feel fine?
I wonder why?
The city started making sounds.
You can see cotton candy clouds
and smell red roses.
I see people.
The birds are flying and the wind is singing
again.
I wonder why?

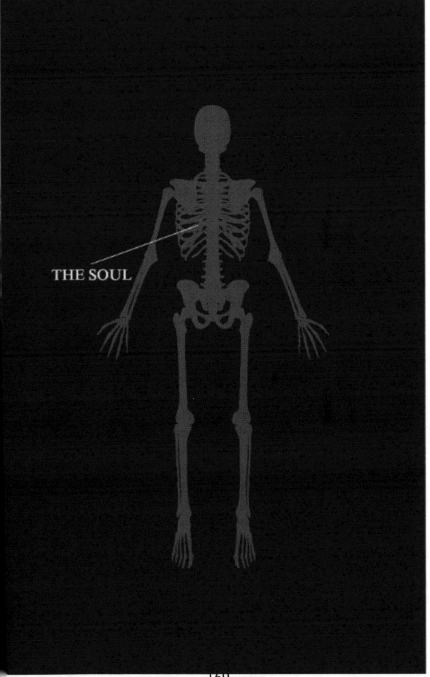

THE SOUL

FAKE SMILE

A fake smile is a smile
even if you have to hide the pain.
Beileve me i've tried.
Give me the oscar.

I GREW UP FOR ME

You really did force me to grow up fast
but I taught myself how to grow up and become a
fun, caring, and loving man.
Someone you didn't care to see
because you stopped growing.

HARD TO FORGET

I forgive them
but I still remember all of it.

SEESAW

I saw my younger self sitting on the seesaw alone.
He was chubby, wearing his favorite striped red
shirt with sweats and shoes from walmart.
I came up to him not sure what to say
but I just knew I had to talk to him today.
We sat on the seesaw going up and down as we
talked about our lives.
He looked up at me
eyes so bright wondering what life's really lik.e
We started to laugh and cry as we shared our
dreams.
I told him about memories and the smiles they
will bring.

I told him to look in the mirror and say *"i love you"*
because it's hard to love something if you can't love
yourself.
I told him you're worth it and not alone
as he listened so closely about my life
and I could see the pain and anger in his eyes but I also
saw a light of hope.
As we both went up and down,
a spark hit me!
That my younger self is still inside of me.
We were the same person with hope in our eyes.
I got off the seesaw with a tear in my eye.
He said
"i love you"
as I watched him grow into me today.

TIME MACHINE

I wish I had a time machine
so I can go back to the time
where I started hating myself
because
it's still hard to
love myself sometimes.
I wish I could of been more
nice to that *"me."*

CLEAR

Nothing prepared me to jump
off a storm cloud
because I had enough rain to build my own
pond.
My eyes could see the lighting that was infront of me as
i'm screaming down
but it didn't hurt me this time.
Not a single scratch on my body.
Not a single tear out of my eyes.
I guess the storm died down
because i'm happy to see the world

clear.

TO THE BOY STARING AT ME

I don't know who I want to be.
I've seen many people walk hills
and paths
to see them become something.
I don't know who I want to be
and i'm scared thinking the world is to big for me.
I've spent my whole life thinking
nobody fucking likes me or want to
see me fall off a bridge
because that's what I wanted to do for so
long
but i'm done with that shit that my mind comes up
with.

Feeding words and ideas inside my head
so the demons inside of me can win.
I don't need to walk the same path as
others or climb some hill
because i've done what I can
and still can't impress a crowd of
people screaming at me as i'm center stage.
They're going to say things that I can't control,
judge me for my mistakes that i make,
and the choices that might make me break.
That's never going to stop
but I can control my mind
and the person that's staring at me in the mirror.

TALKING TO MYSELF

My mind isn't all bad
theirs some good parts to it.
Some is very little
but when it looks out for me
like a 6 year old holding someone's hand,
I am relived that the monsters
are asleep.
As I talk to myself when they aren't
haunting me.

SNAKE VENOM

I've always wondered what life would be if I can read
other peoples minds.
Trust wouldn't be a thing really
and snakes will start spitting venom
when you complement them.
But wouldn't that make me a snake?
I mean sometimes you just want to know what other
people are thinking about you
even if it's good
because my mind likes to think bad
more so good
and theres different kind of snakes
that make up a person.
I never bite
but I mean it when i'm nice.
I don't think bad about them
only question if they want me to die.

HOTEL ROOMS

Even my rooms starts to dispise me.
Nothing really is a safe place
if your room starts to feel like
you overstayed your welcome.

DRIVEWAY

I'm sitting alone on my driveway
thinking about things that I shouldn't be.
People screaming and sounds of shattered glass on the
floor is what I hear in my mind.
Outside I hear the wind and smell the cigarette that the
neighbor just inhaled.
It's dark and cold
something that makes me feel happy
in the moment.
Darkness for when my feelings crawl me into
a cold for when I can start to feel warm as I think about
happy thoughts.
I forgot how to feel.
I forgot how to cry.
I forgot how to think.
As my mind is spinning around
and i'm the horse on the carousel that
my mind is riding.
Never would have thought
that my driveway would
drive me away from myself.

THOUSAND MILES

I run a thousand miles
to get away from this hell that I keep
getting myself into.
I'm coming to rescue him
even if it kills me.
I need one day out from the
darkness,
i'm coming for the light.

JUDGE A BOOK BY ITS COVER

Someone told me Iwas hard to read.
I do bottle in my emotions like when you add
mentos in soda
or when you throw a rock at a piece of glass and it
shatters.
I'm not made up of words for you to read
or showcase pictures with scenes.
I don't even think i've read myself
and never will.

ARTS & CRAFTS

They made me think of things
a child should never think of.
I can't cut parts of my body with a scissor
for them to be happy.
I can't hot glue on a smile when i'm not even
happy, it burns my face.
Staple my mouth shut for words that I wish I
could of said at the moment,
but sharpies are permanent.
Dry erase markers when I wear clothing to make
them appreciate my body.
Glitter on my mind because these thoughts are so
hard to get rid of.
I've ripped my skin like paper
only for it to paint my arms red
and cry watercolor blue.
As crayon wax melts my hair dead
sharpen my nose for a thicker one
because people with big noses look ugly right?
I'm not a kindergarten art project.

IMAGINARY FRIENDS

it's true!
Imaginary friends stay with you till the end.
They still keep the child in you dreaming

THIS PLACE ISN'T BIG FOR THE BOTH OF US

I'm braver when i'm alone
screaming at the world
taking it all out on him.
If I could leave me
I would
but his shadow
will forever haunt me.

HAHA!

When I was younger
my grandpa told me
to just laugh at nothing
everyday.

i've done it ever since

RAINY DAY BLUES

My heartbeat is the thunderstorm
in the world, I feel like I live in.
I love it when it rains as my mood
changes into a rainbow after it rains.
The sun kept me inside because I noticed
people have a lot to say in the light
which is why I come out at night
to feel the cold breeze in between my fingers
with the sky dark
and no sunlight in sight.
I can hide in the dark
but they would scope me in broad daylight
and start telling me how my heartbeat strikes their
living existence
and my looks burn their eyes.
I wish it would be night all the time
so I don't have to see their sun rays
on my body
as I cry thinking
rain is coming my way.
I smile for a split second.

LIVING WITH A SPEAR THROUGH MY SOUL

I took smiling and getting out of my own bed
for granted.

nothing can save me

WHO EVEN CARES?

When I was 8 years old
I ran away from home because my mom
said I couldn't go to school.
I took an old backpack and walked alone to my
nearest elementary school with a bag of doritos in
my left hand and a dream in my right.
I sat at the bench with anger
by the word *"NO"*
not knowing how many times I would
hear that word as I grow up.
I walked back home because I started to feel alone
but once I came back,
no one noticed that I was gone.
No one cared that I was gone.
Who even cares now?

I DON'T MEAN EVERYTHING I SAY

I know I say I hate everybody
and wish to cut ties with every human I
assisoate with.
Go ghost like a boy on the 4'o clock news,
a forgotten police case.
I'm the unsolved mystery of the death of my soul.
I don't need anyone.
I need everyone
and then some.

EVERYTHING HAPPENS FOR A REASON

I used to believe everything happens for a reason
but at this point I can't find a reason
why i'm not allowed to feel like im living a life
that I want to live.
I don't know what I did to deserve this pain.
I wish on every star I see in the night sky
for a new start,
a breath of fresh air
swooping me away from the pain in my heart.
I don't know what to do anymore.

REWRITE

If I had the chance to re write my life
I wouldn't do it.
I needed the challenges and burns on my skin
to be the person I am today.
No means am I perfect
or happy.
I'm breathing in hope
and out negativity.
It honestly doesn't really work
but i'll keep lighting it
no matter how hard it affects my life story.

17

17 I was care free.
I wasn't an adult yet but still felt
like a kid.
Still had random jokes inside of me
and laughs that startle you like a jack in the box.
I was happy.
I got my drivers license like how I dreamt about
driving to wherever I wanted to.
Still in highschool and had the same friends
that I could talk to,
not a single stress in mind.
I was the first leaf that fell when autumn started.
The air was fresh when you breathed,
I loved being 17.

But they don't tell you before that 18,19 you have
to make choices for your future on the spot.
You don't have time to goof around
and cackle at funny tik tok videos.
17 was just a dream
open your eyes back to reality
and suddenly you turn 20.
You're a year closer to dying.
Who was that one friend I used to talk to?
I have memories on my phone, dead end jobs, and
clothes i've outgrown.
I have holes in my pocket,
my parents think i'm stupid.
No i'm feeling kinda lonely.

Back to the thought of nobody knows me anymore.
I don't know what I want but holy shit I want it.
I'm lost, confused, anxious about getting into a good
school.
I'm scared for what's coming up next.
My room doesn't even feel like my room.
I sit in the corner with my headphones on and scream.
I miss being 17

They say these are the golden years of your life but
then why does everyone around me look so lost?

ALONE IN MY CAR

I'm alone in my car
and driving through a tunnel of thoughts
should I keep going or turn back?
Driving towards potched holes on the street
as utility poles mock my dreams.
I keep driving.
I don't know what i'll find.
I'm just waisting time on making myself care.
Should I keep going or turn back?

Street lights are talking,
they are telling me i'm holding on to
grudges.
Stop signs don't exist anymore.
Highways are just excuses to let the GPS
tell you where to go in life
because you don't know yourself.
I'm in the carpool lane to reach my happiness
but no one's sitting but me.

AFTERMATH

All of the crying, breaking, and screaming.
I know it now.

im not alone

UNEXPECTED HIT

Deep sleep at night.
Can't write happy but I hope they feel the
serotonin throbbing.
Can't sleep at night but I can't fight the feeling of
melatonin kicking.

Didn't see it coming this time,
the younger me keeps watching
telling me to *"be more careful next time"*
duck from behind.

A second to late,
it was a jab straight to my soul.
Flew to the gates where angles guard.
They won today
but I can't wait for tomorrow.

I can hear them laugh all around but
most importantly,
he continues to watch
over me.

CAMERA FLASHES

When I fuck things up in life
my mind likes to take photos of
moments that don't need to be captured.
They stay in my mind,
pile up an out of storage dump
on the corner of my brain.
I can't delete them,
they flash when I try.
Stuck in recently deleted
but they tell me,
"at least you're alive."

CURSE WORDS IN CURSIVE

I started this poem on paper
but it turned into me writing curse words in
cursive.
I'm angry and i'm lost.
Texting my friends doesn't count as therapy.
One minute I smile and the next i'm feeling down.
Take me to the hospital.
I'm feeling anxious about the future.
Here's a little pill,
it'll fix it all
but i'm already
hurting my skin
falling off cliffs
holding my breathe.
I used to do these things so
effortlessly.
I continued to write down
curse words in cursive
but stopped writing
the note I would leave on my bed.

TAKING MY OWN ADVICE

They said I should start taking my own
advice
but sometimes I hate myself.
I'mn sorry I don't trust myself.
People call
and I push them away.
I think i'm going insane
but somehow I still cope
with the pain.
Emotional bruises that I cover up
with the sound of rain.

JEALOUSY

I'm jealous of the people who wake up in the
morning with a smile on their face.
I see people getting whatever they want
from brand new cars to clothes that I see myself
wearing.
I can't help that I think about people who don't
even know who I am
but I know they wear different paires of shoes
everyday.
Spray on that expensive cologne that I can smell a
mile away.
Teach me how to smile.
I can't solve this problem without giving up.
I'm jealous of how easy it is for them to talk to
people
while a frog stuck in my throat
won't even make a sound when theirs a crowd full
of randoms that I compare myself to.

BEING A TEENAGER IS BRUTAL

I'm over everyone telling me to enjoy my teenage years
because it's hard.
I'm making choices that are hard to choose
like 10 year old me thinking what puffle I should adopt
on Club Penguin.
My mom still nags me about driving,
I still can't park my car right
one tire crosses the other line.
I forgot how to tie my shoe laces,
"make 2 bunny ears?"
Sorry I still sing the A B C's in my head
because I forget what comes after
H E L P.
I forgot how to make friends with human beings.
I'm scared they think im weird for saying hi,
at least i'm not like the ones that drink and get high.
I feel insecure and feel like everyone hates me.
I make a bitch face and they think i've gone mad.
Sorry that's how my face looks.
Don't even get me started on solving math problems.
$x + y - 5$
I want to fucking die.
Sorry i'm being dramatic,
i'm only a teen.

WINNIE THE POOH

He told me to never forget to grow up and live
happily ever after.
I'm trying to be as sweet as honey.

WHAT I WANT TO BE

I wanted to be a actor when I was 10
then I thought maybe becoming a Starbucks
barista would be fun.
Worked on becoming a cashier at Safeway.
Forced to be a doctor.
Fell in love with writing.
See myself as a business man.
Now i'm not even sure if schools for me.

hey i'm acting...

NYQUIL

Chugging a bottle of nyquil
to help my sudden loss of sleep.
I was scared to dream
as thoughts would rotate around my head.
I'm scared,
don't know if i'll end up dead
in the morning.
I didn't wish to think
i just wanted to sleep
but anxiety keeps rushing
and i've been halusinating
wishing I could throw up
my brain.
As I take another sip of nyquil
begging them to make me sleep.

LEAVES

It's finally the time of year where
leaves change color and fall from trees.
The weather is becoming chilly,
gloomy feels and puddles on streets.
What I would do to be a leaf
that doesn't have any feelings.
Feelings of the fall
nothing to worry about
a free soul being pushed by the wind.
Everyone lies about feeling fine,
now I know why.

STITCHES ON LIPS

I've been silent for so long
that it feels weird saying words
that I wish I said sooner.
A kidnapped soul
that never got to see the world
through a clear lens.
Heavy heart that carries a burden of guilt.
The wounds on my lips aren't healed
but it's time to remove the stitches on my lips.
I'm ready to say things with my chest.

THANK YOU TO MY DEMONS

Thank you to the demons that live in my head,
you taught me how to grow and not be afraid.
With my mind going on a mission of un puzzled
thoughts wishing to be solved.
You tried to eat me alive but I know
you hate me
because you made me hate me to.
I know i've hurt and done some wrong
but i'm trying to make things right again.
I remind myself to breathe because sometimes I
choose to hold in the pain
but i'm still learning to love myself.
Get out of my head
and take the monsters that live in my bed.

LIE WEAK

If you ask me what my poems are about
i'll probably lie
because I don't have the strength inside of me to deny
what has happened to me in my life time.

FOR SEHEJ

I hung up the phone
because it took time to realize I had finally
blocked the ring.
My life was like a lyric
all I had to do was sing.

I have to tell myself to stop caring
for things I can't control
but I would be lying
if I didn't say i've tried to console.

So this is for the bad times
fuck you and your bad vibes.
When I turn 21 i'll make sure to toast myself
and say,
"even if this world feels big for your small things
you matter and one day will see."
I say these 3 words to every one else
so starting today ill start saying it to myself
I love you.

It's kind of cheesy but I have to admit
looking in the mirror and practicing saying it is a
little awkward with eye to eye but i'll keep
practicing like a movie script.
It's my horror movie.
Sehej you're the writer, director, and the actor of
course.

It starts with the word ACTION!

You can feel it in your bones.
You will continue to grow like that blooming red rose.

Through all the upcoming sequels in your life
trust me it'll be worth it till the very end.
The last is paradise
all you have to do is make me your friend.

This ones for Sehej.
Yes this ones for me.

For Sehej.